YOUR KNOWLEDGE HAS VALUE

- We will publish your bachelor's and master's thesis, essays and papers

- Your own eBook and book - sold worldwide in all relevant shops

- Earn money with each sale

Upload your text at www.GRIN.com
and publish for free

Bibliographic information published by the German National Library:

The German National Library lists this publication in the National Bibliography; detailed bibliographic data are available on the Internet at http://dnb.dnb.de .

Imprint:

Copyright © 2006 GRIN Verlag, Open Publishing GmbH
Print and binding: Books on Demand GmbH, Norderstedt Germany
ISBN: 9783640475933

This book at GRIN:

http://www.grin.com/en/e-book/138596/concepts-of-home-and-belonging-in-post-colonial-literature-compared-in-the

Christina Heckmann

Concepts of Home and Belonging in Postcolonial Literature compared in the novels "Small Island" by Andrea Levy and "White Teeth" by Zadie Smith

GRIN Publishing

GRIN - Your knowledge has value

Since its foundation in 1998, GRIN has specialized in publishing academic texts by students, college teachers and other academics as e-book and printed book. The website www.grin.com is an ideal platform for presenting term papers, final papers, scientific essays, dissertations and specialist books.

Visit us on the internet:

http://www.grin.com/

http://www.facebook.com/grincom

http://www.twitter.com/grin_com

Concepts of Home and Belonging in Postcolonial Literature compared in the novels *Small Island* by Andrea Levy and *White Teeth* by Zadie Smith

Schriftliche Hausarbeit

Titel des Seminars: Multiethnic Britain (45142)

Verfasserin:

Christina Heckmann

Eschwege, August, 31st, 2006

Concepts of Home and Belonging in Postcolonial Literature compared in the novels *Small Island* by Andrea Levy and *White Teeth* by Zadie Smith

Contents

1. Introduction

1.1. Brief introduction to home and belonging as a general idea

Home has a significant function in our lives. Thinking of home we associate notions like shelter and comfort and when we come home we want to feel safe and welcome. John McLeod argues in this sense that "to be 'at home' is to occupy a location where we are welcome, where we can be with people very much like ourselves." [1] We are looking for who we are, where we come from and try to find our place in life. When one is born in a country but moves to another where is one's home country then? This question is hard to answer, because migration is always a process which implies a struggle of identities. When the 2nd generation is born in the host country- where do they belong if the host country does not accept them as full members? The term home is highly complicated in a complex and multicultural world like ours.

1.2. Procedure and approach of my analyses

I have centered my term paper on an attempt to identify and characterize the concepts of home and belonging in postcolonial literature.

Comparing how the idea of home and belonging is presented in the novels *White Teeth* by Zadie Smith[2] and *Small Island* by Andrea Levy[3], I have tried a text- extrinsic approach. Furthermore, I have analysed the authors' intentions with regard to the time of publication and the time of the narrative. However, the main aspect of my analyses is which concepts of home and belonging exist and which of them can be found in the novels of my comparison. I have chosen *White Teeth* because it is a novel that deals with the colonial past and the postcolonial present and I have selected *Small Island* because it is a novel that deals with migration in the past. *Small Island* is set at the beginning of migration when many colonized people came to England. Andrea Levy presents different views, the White and Black British point of view at the beginning of migration. My motivation to compare both novels is to go back to the beginning of colonial migration and to show the difference between the concepts from the past to the present.

---

[1] John McLeod, *Beginning Postcolonialism* (Manchester, New York: Manchester University Press, 2000) p. 210.
[2] Zadie Smith, *White Teeth* (London: Penguin Books, 2001), ['2000].
[3] Andrea Levy, *Small Island* (London: Review, Headline Book Publishing, 2004).

2 Theories and concepts of Home and Identity

2.1 Traditional concepts of home and belonging

In this chapter, I focus on home and belonging as a static concept and on home and belonging as a mental construction in the sense of home as a 'mythic place'. At the end of this chapter, I shortly present home and belonging in nationalist representation.

Traditionally home and belonging can be defined as the place where our ancestors used to live, the place of our origin. Consequently, this definition is dedicated to the past without regard where one lives right now. As a result, it is a very passive and static concept, and home is a fixed place. This traditional idea implies that people define their identity according to their roots.

John McLeod argues in this sense:

> The concept of 'home' often performs an important function in our lives. It can act as a valuable means of orientation by giving us a sense of our place in the world. It tells us where we originated from and where we belong.[4]

But so many people have left their homelands in the course of colonization and up to the present time. They have to get along in the host country even though they feel somehow still committed to their old country. Furthermore, for plenty of first generation immigrants it is easier to idealize their home country and see it as the only real home, than to assimilate into the new host country. According to John McLeod, Robert Cohen, Avtar Brah and Salman Rushdie[5] home can be imagined in diaspora communities as a "Mythic Place" or an "Imaginary Homeland".

Migrants see their home country as idyllic place of security and shelter where they are welcome and where the people are like them (race, nationality, religion etc). Migrants often experience discrimination against them in their host country. One way to deal with this experience is to idealize their home country and to see their host country only as a place of temporary residence. As Avtar Brah puts it: "Home is a mythic place of desire in the diasporic imagination."[6] According to this idea home is a mental image:

---

[4] John McLeod, *Beginning Postcolonialism* (Manchester, New York: Manchester University Press, 2000), p. 210.
[5] Cf. ibid., pp. 208-210.
[6] Avtar Brah, *Cartographies of Diaspora: Contesting Identities* (London; New York, Routledge, 1997) p. 192 in John McLeod, *Beginning Postcolonialism* (Manchester, New York: Manchester University Press, 2000), p. 210.

3

In this formulation, home becomes primarily a mental construction built from the incomplete odds and ends of memory that survive from the past. It exists in a fractured, discontinuous relationship with the present.[7]

In this regard, migrants might have an ideal mental image of home, which differs widely from reality. They might have glorified their home so that it might not be possible to return home without disillusion them because their home in reality is not the home of their imagination: "In this sense it is a place of no-return, even if it is possible to visit the geographical territory that is seen as the place of 'origin'."[8]

Home and belonging are important in nationalist representation as well. For example John McLeod describes home as a relevant concept of nationalist representation: "Community, belonging, a sense of rootedness in the land, home- each is relevant to the construction and purpose of nationalist representation."[9] So in a nationalist representation home and belonging are defined in terms of belonging to a nation. This concept of home and belonging can be regarded as an extreme form of traditional concept. According to McLeod "nations are imagined communities and evoke a feeling of belonging, home and community for the people."[10] Furthermore, he argues "every definition of identity is always defined in relation to something else," and "nations place borders that separate the people 'within' from different peoples outside". So according to John McLeod home and belonging in a nationalist representation is bound to the nation one is born in and is defined in relation to other nations whose people have a different identity.

2.2 Fluid concepts- 'Diaspora' Identities

It would be nice and simple if we were all pure. If we all came from where our parents, grandparents and beyond came from. If we all just took on our forefathers'

---

7 John McLeod, *Beginning Postcolonialism* (Manchester, New York: Manchester University Press, 2000), p.211.
[8] Avtar Brah, *Cartographies of Diaspora: Contesting Identities* (London; New York, Routledge, 1997) p. 192. in John McLeod, *Beginning Postcolonialism* (Manchester, New York: Manchester University Press, 2000), p. 210.
[9] John McLeod, *Beginning Postcolonialism* (Manchester, New York: Manchester University Press, 2000), pp.71-72.
[10] Ibid., p.74.

4

culture. Wouldn't it be nice if we could say that all Africans are Black and all English are white?[11]

This quotation by Andrea Levy expresses that in a multicultural world like ours the old static concept does not fit for everybody. There must be the possibility to create new concepts of home and belonging for those people who live in-between cultures.

One very common concept found in postcolonial literature is the concept of 'Diaspora Identity'. In *"Key Concepts in Post-Colonial Studies"* by Bill Ashcroft, Gareth Griffiths and Helen Tiffin the following definition of diaspora can be found: "Diasporas, the voluntary or forcible movement of peoples from their homelands into new regions, is a central historical fact of colonization. [...] The widespread effects of this migration [...] continue on a global scale."[12] John McLeod [13] uses a quotation by Robert Cohen to explain diaspora:

> Diasporas as communities of people living together in one country who 'acknowledge' that 'the old country'- a notion often buried deep in language, religion, custom or folklore-always has some claim on their loyalty and emotions.[14]

Diaspora identities include several generations of immigrants- the first generation immigrants who have experienced migration as well as their descendants who have not experienced migration. Therefore, the term diaspora identities fits better than migrant identities:

"[...] it is more accurate to talk about 'diaspora identities'; not all of those who live in a diaspora, or share an emotional connection to the 'old country', have experienced migration."[15] Diaspora identities can be subdivided into two groups: One group are the first generation immigrants and the other group are their descendants- the second generation immigrants and further generations.

---

[11] Andrea Levy, 'This is my England', The Guardian (February19, 2000) in "'Pivoting the Center':The Fiction of Andrea Levy" by Maria Helena Lima in *Write Black Write British: From Post Colonial to Black British Literature*, ed. by Kadija Sesay (Hertford:Hansib, 2005) p.72.
[12] Bill Ashcroft, Gareth Griffiths; Helen Tiffin, *Key Concepts in Post-Colonial Studies* (London; New York: Routledge, 1998) pp. 68-70.
[13] John McLeod, *Beginning Postcolonialism* (Manchester, New York: Manchester University Press, 2000) p. 207.
[14] Robin Cohen, *Global Diasporas: An Introduction* (UCL Press, 1997) p. ix, in John McLeod, *Beginning Postcolonialism* (Manchester, New York: Manchester University Press, 2000) p. 207.
[15] John McLeod, *Beginning Postcolonialism* (Manchester, New York: Manchester University Press, 2000) p. 207.

The first generation immigrants might glorify their old country and their idea of home can be described as home as a 'mythic place'. [16]

The second generation immigrants might be sub classified as living in-between identities. [17]

As Avtar B rah pu ts it in *Cartographies of Diaspor a: Contesting Identities* (London; New York, Routledge, 1997) p.184:

"All diasporas are differentiated, heterogeneous, contested spaces, even as they are implicated in the construction of a common 'we'."[18]

So diaspora communities consist of heterogeneous identities and are therefore changeable and fluid:

"Differences of gender, 'race', class, religion and language (as well as generational differences) make diaspora spaces dynamic and shifting, open to repeated construction and reconstruction."[19]

2.3 Concept of living 'in-between' identities

The idea of living 'in-between' refers to diaspora identities, who live in-between two cultures- their homeland (where their parents and forefathers used to live in the past) and their place of residence (the land where they live in the present). But mostly they have a clear idea where their home is. John McLeod describes this living in-between position as perilous:

"[...] the perilous intermediate position that *both* migrants and their children are deemed to occupy: living 'in-between' different nations, feeling neither here nor there, [...]."[20] He distinguishes between first and second generation immigrants: "But to children of migrants, the 'interior knowledge' of a distant place is unavailable. Thus, their reflections about these places in terms of 'home' are often differently constructed."[21]

Mainly the term living in-between identity applies to second generation immigrants who have not experienced migration. For example, their parents migrated and they were born in the new country or they were little children when their parents migrated with them. So they have no memories of their parent's homeland so that they cannot see it as their real home. In the new

---

[16] Cf. chapter 2.1 *Traditional Concepts of home and belonging*, p. 2.
[17] Cf. chapter 2.3 *Concept of living 'in-between' identities*, p. 5.
[18] John McLeod, *Beginning Postcolonialism* (Manchester, New York: Manchester University Press, 2000), p. 207.
[19] Ibid., p. 207.
[20] Ibid., p. 214.
[21] Ibid., pp. 212-213.

country, second generation immigrants might not be full integrated although they were born in this country.

2.4 Hybrid identities

According to Bill Ashcroft, Gareth Griffiths and Helen Tiffin, hybridity is one of the most widely employed and most disputed terms in postcolonial theory. "Hybridity commonly refers to the creation of new transcultural forms within the contact zone produced by colonization. As used in horticulture, the term refers to the cross-breeding of two species by grafting or cross- pollination to form a third, 'hybrid' species."[22] "Hybridity has frequently been used in post-colonial discourse to mean simply cross-cultural 'exchange'"[23]. The 'cross-cultural exchange', which is mentioned in the quotation, means that cultures are mingled and multiplied. According to Homi K. Bhabha "all cultural statements and systems are constructed in a space that he calls the 'Third Space of enunciation' (1994: 37). Cultural identity always emerges in this contradictory and ambivalent space [...]"[24]. So Identity is formed by numerous sources. It is not prescribed and it is not a fixed notion. The border that migrants have to cross is an opportunity for new, hybrid forms of identity and knowledge. It is a point of transition- the third space where past and present– old and new mingles until borders are dissolved and a clear delimitation and classification of identities is not possible anymore.

3. Migration and home- the importance of home in *Small Island*

Migration means to leave one's home behind and according to Roy Sommer "Fictions of Migration"[25] often deal with the problems and hopeless situation of the immigrants in their host country, which is also called "exile".

In *Small Island,* we find only one generation of immigrants, the protagonists Hortense and Gilbert. They are both from Jamaica, Gilbert half Jamaican-half English and Hortense not as black as other Jamaicans but "born with a golden skin"[26]. They left their home Jamaica to start a new life in England. First, it is Celia Langley, Hortense's friend at the teacher- training college in Kingston, who dreams of leaving Jamaica and living in England when she is older. In her

---

[22] Bill Ashcroft, Gareth Griffiths; Helen Tiffin, *Key Concepts in Post-Colonial Studies* (London; New York: Routledge, 1998), p. 118.
[23] Ibid., p. 119.
[24] Ibid., p. 118.
[25] Roy Sommer, *Fictions of Migration: Ein Beitrag zur Theorie und Gattungstypologie des zeitgenössischen, interkulturellen Romans in Großbritannien*, (Trier:WVT, 2001), p. 78.
[26] Andrea Levy, *Small Island*, p. 527.

imagination she lives in a big house with a bell at the front door and she dreams of ringing this bell.[27] But it is Hortense for whom this dream comes true in the end. In Jamaica Hortense makes a deal with Gilbert, a Jamaican who fought in the RAF for England in the Second World War. He wants to go back to England and Hortense gives him the money for the journey to England. In return he has to marry her so that she can leave Jamaica as a married woman. But her first impression is: "'Just this? Just this? You bring me all this way for just this?'"[28] She had longed to find a better life in England. She sees England as her destiny and dreams of a modest house: "'A starched tablecloth embroidered with bows. Armchairs in the sitting room placed around a small wood fire. The house is modest- nothing fancy, no show- the kitchen small but with everything I need to prepare meals.'"[29] But in England she has to face the harsh reality: "I never dreamed England would be like this. So cheerless. Determined."[30] The accommodation Gilbert found for them to live in was not what Hortense had expected: The house is run down, only a dim light in the corridor with windows missing. So contrary to her expectation Hortense has to live in this shabby house as Queenie Bligh's lodger.

Furthermore Andrea Levy describes Gilbert's first impression and feelings in England very detailed in the following passage:

> [...] these were the first weeks for we Jamaicans. And every one of us was fat as a Bible with faith that we would get a nice place to live in England-a bath, a kitchen, a little patch of garden. These two damp cramped rooms that the friend of Winston's brother had let us use were temporary. [...] Better than the hostel. Two months I was there! Two months, and this intimate hospitality had begun to violate my hope. I needed somewhere so I could start to live. [31]

Andrea Levy, whose father also arrived in Britain aboard the SS Empire Windrush in 1948, describes the hopes and dreams of Gilbert and the other Jamaicans as very strong at the beginning, but after two month he begins to lose hope. In this passage she also describes that finding a place to make one's

---

[27] Andrea Levy, *Small Island*, p. 11.
[28] Ibid., p. 21.
[29] Ibid., pp. 100-101.
[30] Ibid., p. 225.
[31] Ibid., p. 214.

home and feel at home is necessary for living. Gilbert needs a place where he could start to live.

In the end Gilbert and Hortense manage it to fulfil their dreams. They get the opportunity to move into a house, which is shabby and broke because of the war as well, but for small rent. They are very optimistic. Even Hortense says, "'These things can be fix up.'[…] 'With a little paint and some carpet. […] You will see– we will make it nice.'"[32]. Gilbert is confident as well that he and Hortense, who is always well-dressed with a hat and clean, white gloves, manage to make their sweet home in England. He "would make this life around her good enough to fit that fine apparel."[33] So here the importance of home is emphasised. Hortense and Gilbert feel like they have found their place, their home in England. And after Hortense showed Gilbert some affection and let him sleep in the bed with her, Gilbert feels as happy as can be. "At that moment if the Caribbean sun had been shining on me, while naked girls fanned me with banana leaves, it could not have felt any more pleasant."[34]

4. Traditional concepts of home and belonging in *Small Island* and in *White Teeth*

We can find old concepts of home and belonging in *Small Island*. Elwood, a Jamaican, is a boyhood friend of Gilbert and both men wanted to make money with beekeeping. But after they unfortunately lost all the bees they talked about their plans for the future: Elwood wants to fight for an independent Jamaica. In his opinion, a Jamaican should stay in his home country where he was born and fight for his country as well.

"'And you a Jamaican. You born a Jamaican. You die a Jamaican. Jamaica mean nothing to ya, man? Why you wan'leave?'"[35] But he concludes that it is not surprising to him that Gilbert will go back to England because Gilbert is only half Jamaican: "'You may look like one of us but not'in'gon'change the fact your daddy is a white man.'"[36] So here we can find the nationalist representation of home and belonging. In Elwood's opinion home and belonging are defined in terms of belonging to a nation where one is born in- where one's roots are. Therefore, Levy presents a nationalist concept in the

---

[32] Andrea Levy, *Small Island*, pp. 503-504.
[33] Ibid., p. 503.
[34] Ibid., p. 505.
[35] Ibid., p. 208.
[36] Ibid., p.209.

character of Elwood: A Jamaican who is born in Jamaica as child of pure
Jamaicans belongs to Jamaica and his home cannot be elsewhere in the world.
In contrast to Elwood we find furthermore other characters in *Small Island* who
have also traditional ideas of home and belonging. For example, we can find
the traditional idea of home as a 'Mythic Place' or an 'Imaginary Homeland'[37]:
As Andrea Levy emphasises, "Remembering always brings its share of pain to
African Diasporan peoples- in Jamaica or in London."[38]

In *Small Island,* it is Gilbert Joseph who in the following passage recalls his
sweet home Jamaica and wonders if his decision to go back to Britain was
right.

> Perhaps Elwood was right. 'Stay in Jamaica', he had begged me. […] My boyhood
> friend, what was passing before his eye now in the Caribbean island? Sitting on the
> veranda, he was watching the Jamaican sun as, lowering, the sky glowed purple
> orange blue pink. Sucking on soursop, the juice sticky on his chin, the flesh fat
> between his teeth. [39]

In addition to the concept of home as a "Mythic Place", we can find another
static, traditional concept of home and belonging in the novel. Gilbert and his
wife Hortense have a static, traditional idea of home and belonging in the sense
of belonging to the 'Mother country' England. Seen in this light Hortense and
Gilbert are 'Children of the Empire' who come home to the 'Mother
country'[40].

Gilbert joins the RAF to fight for England against Hitler in the Second World
War. When other British or American soldiers wonder about seeing a coloured
man in a British uniform he explains:

> 'I am from Jamaica but England is my Mother Country. […] 'Britain is Jamaica's
> Mother Country. But we are all part of the Empire.' […] 'The British own the
> island of Jamaica, it is in the Caribbean Sea and we, the people of Jamaica, are all
> British because we are her subjects.'[…] 'I am a volunteer for the war effort. Here
> to help the Mother Country.'[41]

---

[37] Cf. chapter 2.1 *'Traditional' concepts of home and belonging,* p. 2.
[38] Andrea Levy, unpublished interview, 2002 in "'Pivoting the Center':The Fiction of Andrea
Levy" by Maria Helena Lima in *Write Black Write British: From Post Colonial to Black
British Literature,* ed. by Kadija Sesay (Hertford:Hansib, 2005), p.75.
[39] Andrea Levy, *Small Island,* p. 325.
[40] Andrea Levy, unpublished interview, 2002 in "'Pivoting the Center':The Fiction of Andrea
Levy" by Maria Helena Lima in *Write Black Write British: From Post Colonial to Black
British Literature,* ed. by Kadija Sesay (Hertford:Hansib, 2005), p.75.
[41] Andrea Levy, *Small Island,* pp. 156-158.

Therefore, Gilbert has a very positive view of belonging to an English colony. He is proud to belong to the Mother Country England and wants to fight for England. He considers himself British because Jamaica is a British colony. So his idea of home and belonging is static and traditional in the sense of belonging to the place of origin- Jamaica which belongs to England.

Hortense also feels English and sees England as her home. She expresses this idea when she speaks of England as her destiny: "I determined then to make this place somewhere I could live- if only for this short while. For England was my destiny."[42] Furthermore, she tries to adopt the English lifestyle. For example she tries to speak the language properly: "Whereas I, since arriving in this country, had determined to speak in an English manner."[43]

Even if Smith's novel was published earlier than Levy's *Small Island*, *White Teeth* is set in the present whereas Levy goes back to the beginning of postcolonial migration, when the numbers of colonised people around the world, who came to Britain, increased after the end of the Second World War. "In Britain, colonial peoples were specifically recruited by the Government to cope with labour shortages, such as the drive after the Second World War to employ Caribbeans in public services like health and transport."[44]

Smith presents in her novel a mixture of nationalities and generations. She illustrates new concepts of defining one's identity and argues: "'And if people are going to be able to deal with the fact that they are not who they were a generation before, and their children are not going to be like that, you have to try to have some understanding that difference is okay.'"[45] However, she also illustrates old, static concepts in contrast to new fluid concepts:

For example Samad, who is first generation immigrant, is a character in *White Teeth* with a traditional idea of home. He is the head of the Bangladeshi Iqbal-family who migrated to England with his wife Alsana and who idealizes his home country Bangladesh.. It is clear for him that Bangladesh is his home. He tends to glorify his homeland in his temporary residence England and sees his home country as a 'mythic place of desire'[46].

[42] Ibid., p. 226.
[43] Ibid., p.449.
[44] John McLeod, *Beginning Postcolonialism* (Manchester, New York: Manchester University Press, 2000) p.206.
[45] Benedicte Page, 'Chewing up the past', *The Bookseller* (October 15, 1999).
[46] Cf. chapter 2.1 *Traditional Concepts of Home*, p. 2

Samad illustrates very well that plenty of immigrants feel somewhere deep inside that they belong to their country of origin. As Samad describes it: "'[…] it feels to me like you make a devil's pact when you walk into this country. You hand over your passport at the check-in, you get stamped, you want to make a little money, get yourself started…but you mean to go back!'"[47] Therefore, Samad, like plenty of immigrants intends to go back, but only a few manage to return. Samad describes the host country as a "'[…] place where you are never welcomed, only tolerated. […] Like you are an animal finally house trained.'"[48] In this sentence, he compares immigrants like him to wild, savage animals who were trained to live in a house, Britain, eventually, but even after this domestication, the British only tolerate them. Furthermore, he poses the question: "'Who would want to stay?'" and he concludes: "'But you have made a devil's pact…it drags you in and suddenly you are unsuitable to return, your children are unrecognizable, you belong nowhere.'" He describes here a feeling of being stuck between two worlds- his place of residence, Britain and his glorified home, Bangladesh. All this leads to an identity crisis and finally, he does not know where he belongs but he wants to go back to his home:

"I wish to live as I was always meant to! I wish to return to the East! […] I should never have come here- that's where every problem has come from. Never should have brought my sons here, so far from God."[49] Samad like many other immigrants sees himself for ever only as visitor of the host country who always intended to go back to the place he still considers home. So here, we find a static concept of home.

Archie Jones also has a more static and traditional idea of home and belonging. He philosophizes about dying right before trying to commit suicide: "The way Archie saw it, country people should die in the country and city people should die in the city. Only proper. In death as he was in life and all that."[50] I think one could see in this remark that one should die where he was born and therefore one could argue this would consequently mean no movement.

---

[47]Zadie Smith, *White Teeth,* p.407.
[48] Ibid., p.407.
[49] Zadie Smith, *White Teeth,* p.145.
[50] Zadie Smith, *White Teeth,* p 3.

5. Fluid concepts- 'diaspora identities', living 'in-between identities' and 'hybrid identities' in *White Teeth* compared to 'in-between identities' in *Small Island*

Primarily Smith reveals that old static concepts, which are bound only to one's roots, must be substituted because they are inadequate and old-fashioned for many people.

Tracey L. Walters wrote about Zadie Smith:

> Smith reveals that in today's postmodern millennial world, notions of ethnic and racial identity cannot be defined in terms of ancestry, language or culture because the cultural hybridisation of English society has made concepts of ethnicity and race indeterminate.[51]

For example, the concept of diaspora identities is one fluid concept that can be found in *White Teeth*. It includes several generations: First of all Samad and Alsana are diaspora identities. They belong to the first generation immigrants and tend to glorify their home Bangladesh in the sense of Home as 'mythic place of desire' which is a static concept. Secondly the concept of diaspora identities also includes their offspring who could be considered as living 'in-between' identities.

For the second generation it is difficult to define where they come from. Zadie Smith illustrates in-between identities for different characters and their struggle with their feeling of belonging very clearly in her novel and gives several examples. I have focused on two characters of *White Teeth* here. Millat is a good example of in-between-identity. He is trapped between his parent's home country Bangladesh and England. For him the question of belonging is very hard to answer. He does not know were he belongs:

> He knew that he, Millat was a Paki no matter were he came from; that he smelt of curry; had no sexual identity; took other peoples jobs;[...] In short, he knew he had no face in this country, no voice in this country, until the week before last when suddenly people like Millat were on every channel and every radio and every newspaper and they were angry, and Millat recognised the anger, thought it recognized him, and grapped it with both hands.[52]

---

[51] Tracey L. Walters *"We're All English Now Mate Like it or Lump It": The Black/Britishness of Zadie Smith's White Teeth"* in *Write Black Write British: From Post Colonial to Black British Literature*, ed. by Kadija Sesay (Hertford:Hansib, 2005).
[52] Zadie Smith, *White Teeth*, p.234.

So Millat experienced that he, although he was born in England and has lived there all his life, is not accepted and will never be accepted as English. He is insulted and discriminated against, although he wears western clothes (Nike) and assimilates to the western world. This leads to identity crises. In his search for identity and belonging, he joins the fundamental Muslim group called K.E.V.I.N. He feels that this group can give him an identity and can explain the world to him. This group also wears real uniforms, so the feeling of belonging to this group is strengthened. Ironically, Millat turns out a fundamental Muslim never having visited Bangladesh and Magid, being send to Bangladesh to become a good Muslim turns out to become very English.

Furthermore Irie, a central character, is also a living 'in-between' identity. She is the daughter of Archie and Clara Jones and she is half- English and half-Jamaican. She feels trapped between her Jamaican genes and her wish to be English. "But Irie didn't know she was fine. There was England, a gigantic mirror, and there was Irie, without reflection. A stranger in a stranger land."[53] She is in love with Millat who only likes English girls and she is very unhappy that she has "Hortense's substantial Jamaican frame."[54] Therefore, she longs to be English although she identifies neither with her English roots nor with her Jamaican roots. Suffering from unrequited love to Millat, she tries to change her hair into "Straight straight long black sleek flickable tossable shakeable touchable finger-through-able wind-blowable hair. With a fringe."[55]. She hopes that Millat might fall in love with her when she looks more like an English girl. But her attempt to change her hair in a Willesden salon failed.

Through the whole novel Irie struggles with her identity. She feels first "in-between", and then she wants to look like an English girl because of Millat. Later she tries to get back to her roots:

> Why bother when there was now this other place? (For Jamaica appeared to Irie as if it were newly made. Like Columbus himself, just by discovering it she had brought it into existence.) [...] a place where things simply *were*. No fictions, no myths, no lies, no tangled webs- this is how Irie imagined her homeland.[...] And the particular magic of *homeland*, its particular spell over Irie, was that it sounded like a beginning.[56]

---

[53]Ibid. p 266.
[54]Zadie Smith, *White Teeth*, p 265.
[55] Ibid., p.273
[56] Ibid., p. 402.

In the end Irie is pregnant without knowing who the father is because she had sex with both Iqbal twins, but she seems to have found paradise and freedom. Smith wrote "Irie has seen a time, a time not far from now, when roots won't matter any more because [...] they're too long and they're too tortuous and they're just buried too damn deep."[57]

She gives up the idea of belonging and waits for a world where the idea of belonging does not matter anymore. Therefore, the concept of Hybridity [58] can be found in Irie's unborn child. The child is described as "fatherless little girl [...] a puppet clipped of paternal strings"[59] who can never be mapped exactly:

> "'But it asked too much of her. It requires her to go back, back, back to the root, to the fundamental moment when sperm met egg, when egg met sperm-so early in this history it cannot be traced. Irie's child can never be mapped exactly nor spoken of with any certainty.'"[60]

Compared to *White Teeth* Andrea Levy shows more the old static order. But this is not surprising because Small Island is a historical novel which is set in the past. In *White Teeth* we find three generations of immigrants. *Small Island* shows us only first generation immigrants of whom only Gilbert is half-Jamaican and half-English and therefore one could argue that he is an 'in-between' identity. Nevertheless, he feels English because he considers Jamaica as part of England.[61] Therefore, I would rather not consider him an 'in-between' identity.

In the end of *Small Island* we can find another character who could be considered an 'in between' identity. The mixed-race baby Michael is born in a time full of prejudices. He is half English and half Jamaican. His mother Queenie seemed not to care about society gossip, social pressure and her neighbour's prejudices against foreigners when she took black lodgers in her house. She defies all the social pressure and helps black immigrants. But in the end she gives her coloured baby away probably because she wants to protect the baby and to spare her husband feeling. "I just want him with people

---

[57] Zadie Smith, *White Teeth*, p. 527.
[58] cf. 2.4 *Hybrid identities*
[59] Ibid., p. 541
[60] Ibid., p.527.
[61] Cf. Chapter 4, *Traditional Concepts of Home and Belonging in Small Island and White Teeth*

who'll understand. Can't you see? His own kind. [...] I know you could give him a better life than I ever could."[62]

But strictly speaking Levy does not specially present fluid concepts of home and belonging in her novel.

6. Conclusion and outlook

It is not possible to have a clear-cut definition of home and belonging and it is impossible to define a concept of home and belonging which fits for everyone. In addition to the static, traditional concept of home and belonging more fluid concepts are needed. Especially in postcolonial literature the question of home and belonging is often an issue for example as presented in this term paper in *Small Island* and particularly in *White Teeth*. Many immigrants of all generations have problems with their identity in their new country.

> Questions as to roots and origin haunt the imaginations of disparate peoples across national and intercontinental boundaries, questions as to one's (identity) and identification with a particular fellow person, group, society, ethnicity, nation/nationality and the like seem to puzzle human beings more and more.[63]

Regarding both novels it is interesting that Andrea Levy, writing her novel *Small Island* after Zadie Smith's *White Teeth* was published, shows us traditional ideas of home and belonging. One would expect that, after Zadie Smith has created a very optimistic view about a multicultural society with her novel *White Teeth*, other British-born black writers like Andrea Levy would continue at this level and include Zadie Smith's fluid ideas of home and belonging in their writing. Especially Smith's vision of a time, when roots are not important anymore because nobody can be mapped exactly, raises the hope that nationalistic views, like "being British means being White" will become obsolete. But the concept of hybridity is illustrated in *White Teeth* very one-sided because only the positive aspects are mentioned. However, hybrid identities and the idea of a time "when roots won't matter any more"[64] also have negative aspects: "This is not to deny that the city (London) is still blighted with racism. Integration is not equality."[65] So even if one sees oneself as hybrid identity and is integrated there is still racism, discrimination and

---

[62] Andrea Levy, *Small Island*, p.522.
[63] Susanne Pichler, *Buchi Emecheta's London Novels: An intercultural Approach* (Trier: WVT,2001), p.40.
[64] Zadie Smith, *White Teeth*, p. 527.
[65] Yasmin Alibhai-Brown, *A magic carpet of cultures in London: on the city's new arts scene, racial barriers crumble and outsiders crowd inside* (The New York Times, June 25,2000, British Council Newspaper Database, Thomas Gale, 30 November 2005), p.3.

problems between cultures and religions. "You see mixed –race couples everywhere and friendships too. But you know how access is still denied and what the struggles are. We are nowhere near the post-racial London depicted in Zadie's book (*White Teeth*)."[66]

Nevertheless, it is very encouraging to read *White Teeth* and compared to Andrea Levy's presentation of migration at the beginning of postcolonial migration it shows a progress which should be continued in the future. Furthermore, *Small Island* like *White Teeth* gives the reader an optimistic, positive view of home and belonging especially after "much of the fiction of the 1980s appears pessimistic about the possibility of belonging."[67] Gilbert and Hortense feel that they belong to the British Empire and they feel at home in England at the end:

> After reading *Small Island*, moreover, readers will not be able to see 'home' and 'empire' as two separate spaces, leaving unchallenged the fiction of a pre-existing England, herself constituted outside and without imperialism.[68]

Both authors reveal that it is particularly important to have fluid concepts and to see home and belonging not as a fixed static idea because one's identity and therefore one's idea of home and belonging can change through life and can be re-created. In *White Teeth* we can find a good example on which I have focused in chapter 5. Irie's idea of home and belonging changes: The static concept of roots does not fit for her because she neither identifies with her Jamaican nor with her English roots. She feels in-between and struggles with her identity. Trying to get back to her roots she fails and is happy in the end with the concept of hybridity. Even if fluid concepts are not predominant in *Small Island*, reading Andrea Levy's novels require a progressive way of thinking of identity as well:

> Instead of thinking of identity as an already accomplished fact, which the new cultural practices would then represent, Levy's novels require that we think of identity as a "production," as Stuart Hall writes, which is "never complete, always in process, and always constituted within, not outside, representation.[69]

---

[66] Ibid., p. 4.
[67] Maya Jaggi, 'Redefining Englishness', in: *W. Waterstone's Magazine 6* (1996), p. 68.
[68] Maria Helena Lima, 'Pivoting the Center':The Fiction of Andrea Levy" in *Write Black Write British: From Post Colonial to Black British Literature*, ed. by Kadija Sesay (Hertford:Hansib, 2005), pp. 56-57.
[69] Ibid, p. 58.

To conclude this term paper both novels deal with the concept of home and belonging, different concepts are presented and an immense progress has been made. The old static concept has been extended and fluid concepts have been defined. To define ones roots can help to form ones identity, but it is dangerous to think only in those terms because to hold on one's roots too strong could paralyse. Moreover it is important to see home and belonging (identity) as a production according to Stuart Hall as cited above.

Literaturverzeichnis:

Primärliteratur:

Levy, Andrea, *Small Island*, (London: Review, Headline Book Publishing, 2004).

Smith, Zadie, *White Teeth,* (London: Penguin Books, 2001, first published by Hamish Hamilton Ltd, 2000).

Sekundärliteratur:

Alibhai-Brown, Yasmin, *Imagining the New Britain* (New York: Routledge, 2001).

Ashcroft, Bill; Gareth Griffiths; Helen Tiffin, *Key Concepts in Post-Colonial Studies* (London; New York, Routledge, 1998).

Brah, Avtar, *Cartographies of Diaspora: Contesting Identities* (London; New York, Routledge,1997).

Cohen, Robin, *Global Diasporas: An Introduction* (UCL Press, 1997).

Gilroy, Paul, *The Black Atlantic* (Verso, 1993).

Jaggi, Maya, *"Redefinning Englishness"* in *W. Waterstone's Magazine* 6 (1996), p. 63.

Jaggi, Maya, *"The new Brits on the block",* *The Guardian* (July13, 1996).

Lima, Maria Helena, *"'Pivoting the Center':The Fiction of Andrea Levy"* in *Write Black Write British: From Post Colonial to Black British Literature*, ed. by Kadija Sesay (Hertford:Hansib, 2005).

McLeod, John *Beginning Postcolonialism* (Manchester, New York: Manchester University Press, 2000).

Mercer, Kobena *Welcome to the Jungle: New Positions in Black Culture Studies* (New York: Routledge, 1994).

Page, Benedicte *'Chewing up the past',* *The Bookseller* (October 15, 1999).

Sommer, Roy, *Fictions of Migration: Ein Beitrag zur Theorie und Gattungstypologie des zeitgenössischen, interkulturellen Romans in Großbritannien*, (Trier: WVT, 2001).

Walters, Tracey L., *"We're All English Now Mate Like it or Lump It"*: *The Black/Britishness of Zadie Smith's White Teeth"* in *Write Black Write British: From Post Colonial to Black British Literature*, ed. by Kadija Sesay (Hertford: Hansib, 2005).

Pichler, Susanne, *Buchi Emecheta's London Novels: An intercultural Approach* (Trier: WVT,2001)